CUT TO THE CHASE

REAL ESTATE GUIDE

LINDA PRETRE

LifeRich
PUBLISHING®

This book is a work of non-fiction. Unless otherwise noted, the author
and the publisher make no explicit guarantees as to the accuracy of
the information contained in this book and in some cases, names of
people and places have been altered to protect their privacy.

LifeRich Publishing is a registered trademark of
The Reader's Digest Association, Inc.

LifeRich Publishing books may be ordered through booksellers or by contacting:

LifeRich Publishing
1663 Liberty Drive
Bloomington, IN 47403
www.liferichpublishing.com
844-686-9607

Because of the dynamic nature of the Internet, any web addresses or
links contained in this book may have changed since publication and
may no longer be valid. The views expressed in this work are solely those
of the author and do not necessarily reflect the views of the publisher,
and the publisher hereby disclaims any responsibility for them.

Any people depicted in stock imagery provided by Getty Images are
models, and such images are being used for illustrative purposes only.
Certain stock imagery © Getty Images.

ISBN: 978-1-4897-3231-6 (sc)
ISBN: 978-1-4897-3232-3 (e)

Print information available on the last page.

LifeRich Publishing rev. date: 02/18/2021

To my husband, John, for being a wonderful partner in life and real estate.

Also to all the real estate buffs, investors, agents, and other professionals or wannabes.

"As a seasoned investor and landlord, Linda is keenly aware of the pitfalls and opportunities that almost always present themselves in any real estate deal. Over time, she has developed a systematic approach that guides her as she analyzes the pros and cons of each and then how best to proceed. If you are thinking of dipping your toe into the world of real estate, or simply want to learn more about it, Linda will be an invaluable source of insight from someone that has "been there and done that"!"

Rick Wunderlich - Realtor Keller Williams Realty - Chesterfield

Linda Pretre's many years as a successful real estate investor come together in the Real Estate Guide. The guide is set up in easy-to-follow steps that take you from idea to investment. Linda has set the guide up in such a way that whether you're a novice or a seasoned investor you'll find valuable information to help you in building your real estate portfolio.

Jill McCoy, Keller Williams Realty
Real Estate professional and educator

CONTENTS

PREFACE

Through my experiences, good and bad, I share the insights in this book that I wished I'd had when I started out. You can learn from my trials, mistakes, and successes. This book gives you points and lists to absorb and refer to continually as you personalize your real estate journey to your needs and goals.

SECTION 1

REAL ESTATE GUIDE

CHAPTER 1

REAL ESTATE TEAM

Real estate gurus and investors need a great real estate team to perform all the functions necessary to carry out your business. Your team should consist of at least the following professionals:

1. Real estate agent
2. Lender
3. Insurance agent
4. Title/closing company
5. Appraiser
6. Inspector
7. Contractor
8. Handyman
9. Attorney
10. Accountant
11. Property manager (or you can manage yourself)
12. Tenant screener
13. Mentor

Keeping your properties with the same agent or agency normally affords you the best commission rate available.

Shop your mortgage and title costs and be sure to get the best deal from a reputable company.

Make sure you detail all items that need to be done, including costs in contracts. Make sure to get everything in writing because verbal agreements do not hold up under legal scrutiny or in court.

Pay contractors very soon after they finish; they will likely prioritize your work and respond when you need them in the future.

Make sure your attorney and accountant are familiar with real estate and/or real estate investing so they can advise you and handle your legal issues and taxes appropriately.

If you can, manage your own properties. It will save you money.

Screen your tenants thoroughly and talk to the prospects. Make sure they provide all the documents you are requesting. If they do not, move on.

Enlist the help of a mentor to show you the ropes and the good, bad, and ugly aspects of real estate. Most mentors who have been in the business for years will have stories in all the categories above.

TIPS FOR BUYING AND SELLING

My best advice is to buy the property right! I cannot stress this one enough!

Also consider the following:

1. Buy right (below market value).
2. Pay the mortgage down.
3. Pay off (increase cash flow).
4. Solve buyer/seller's problem/need.
5. Buy when the market is down.
6. Sell when the market is up.

Find out the buyer/seller's needs and why he or she is looking to buy or sell. If you can meet those needs, you could get closer to a deal.

Buy with other people's (a lender's) money. If you get appreciation, you may be able to refinance, increase value to the property even more, or sell higher than what you bought for. We will cover increasing value later in the book.

The seller pays commission to the real estate agent.

To get the best price, here are several questions to consider:

1. Is the property for investment or for owner-occupied use?
2. How many units are in the deal?
3. How much are you putting down on the property?
4. Is there a security deposit involved?
5. Is there option money involved?
6. What types of financing are being considered?
7. Is a preapproval available?
8. How long will the closing take?
9. Are there any contract addendums or adjustments?
10. Is this a cash deal?
11. Do you want to consider a contract addendum or extension?

Before you buy or sell, getting to know various aspects about the property and the area is crucial:

1. Location
2. Condition
3. Value
4. Amenities
5. Income potential
6. Financing options

Make sure you consider all costs involved in buying/selling, including

1. acquisition;
2. transaction;
3. closing;
4. repair;
5. holding;
6. selling.

As you look at costs, take these steps:

1. Determine the purchase price based on comps (start with market value based on comparables from the real estate agent).
2. Add what you want to make on the deal or what equity you want to gain.
3. Deduct renovation and repair costs.
4. Factor in the cost of the sale, including holding and closing costs.

Next, assess if you need any escape clauses in your offer. These might include

1. inspection;
2. financing;
3. repairs;
4. other party approval.

If the deal is not good or the terms are not what you want, you or your agent can set up contingencies or you can walk away before the deal is complete!

CHAPTER 3

PROCESS AND STRATEGY

You should make money when you buy the property! Consider the following strategies to buy the property right:

1. Buy a distressed property.
2. Buy from a motivated seller.
3. Get the best deal on terms.
4. Let the other party offer first.
5. Buy and sell as the market dictates.
6. Buy with little money down.
7. Look for deals that may be hiding or not readily available.

You could join a real estate club or education group, but be careful with certain people; you never know their motivations.

Also consider working with a role model or mentor, but again be careful that they do not take advantage of you and that they have your best interests at heart.

Always remember that you must take action to make something happen. The following tips will help you along your journey.

1. Manage your time, including phone and email.
2. Enlist help from others.
3. Use the internet to your advantage.
4. Get disciplined.
5. Ask yourself if the activity you are doing is helping you achieve your goals.
6. Always strive to get closer to your goals.
7. Your goals should be written, realistic, and measurable.
8. Visualize yourself achieving your goals.
9. Make a plan and work toward it.

Here are some ways to achieve your goals:

1. Have a written strategy.
2. Be determined.
3. Be persistent.
4. Get organized, including your desk and documents.
5. Be knowledgeable and focused.
6. Manage your time wisely.
7. Keep good records.
8. Update the process when necessary.
9. Take action!

Make a plan and follow it. Here are some tips to accomplish that:

1. Make a to-do list for the day.
2. Do the most important task first.
3. Use technology to be efficient.
4. Obtain assistance when needed, such as with legal and accounting issues.
5. Do what leads toward your goals.

Some strategies for real estate include

1. buy and hold,
2. wholesale,
3. flip.

When it comes to marketing yourself, make sure your real estate business card is unique. Consider putting your focus on the card, such as "real estate investor specializing in rentals or flipping." Make sure you hand out the cards to get the word out.

You can also attract renters and buyers through real estate that has these desirable characteristics:

1. Great neighborhood or location
2. Close to transportation
3. Close to shopping and schools
4. In a great school district
5. Spacious
6. Clean
7. Updated
8. Affordable
9. Has a garage or storage area
10. Great amenities

REAL ESTATE BENEFITS

There are many benefits to doing real estate:

1. Using other people's money
2. Using other people's time
3. Little to no upfront investment
4. Cash flow
5. Control of the asset
6. Making money without needing to tend to the property every day (i.e., passive income)
7. Appreciation
8. Increased equity
9. Tax benefits such as deductions and depreciation
10. Tax-free exchanges
11. Can replace your day job
12. Can help with retirement or accelerate retirement
13. Freedom

Real estate always has value, and normally it increases over time.

You can also deduct many things as expenses or on your taxes. Be sure you are considering the following possibilities for deductions:

1. Interest
2. Maintenance
3. Management
4. Travel
5. Dining
6. Legal
7. Insurance
8. Advertising
9. Utilities
10. Tools/supplies
11. Phone/internet
12. Office
13. Postage
14. Commissions
15. Mileage

CHAPTER 5

REAL ESTATE FINANCES

It is important to be knowledgeable about finances, lending, and taxes. I recommend working with professionals in these areas who have experience with real estate.

You can avoid capital gains taxes on a sale of a rental if you do a 1031 exchange or you've lived in the property for two of the last five years.

Keep in mind that the appreciation that normally occurs over time can lead to increased value, which can lead to increased cash flow and profit.

Everyone needs a place to live even in rough times.

To protect your assets, consider a limited liability company (LLC), and do a transfer upon death with the LLC. Also consider an umbrella insurance policy, especially if you are refinancing or selling.

Make sure you have separate bank accounts for personal and business and for different businesses.

Consider the following types of real estate investments:

1. Lease option
2. Foreclosure
3. Preforeclosure
4. Rental
5. Real estate owned (REO)
6. Short sale
7. Tax sale or lien

Accelerate payments on rentals to pay less interest and potentially use money from a home equity line of credit (HELOC) or other loan that uses simple interest rather than amortized interest like a mortgage. This will save you money.

The benefits of paying off a mortgage early and accelerating the payments are multifold:

1. Increase cash flow.
2. Decrease interest paid.
3. Reduce debt.
4. Gain financial independence.
5. Reduce stress.
6. Increase credit score.

Here is a step-by-step example of how to accelerate payments:

1. Open a HELOC or line of credit.
2. Pull $9,000 from the HELOC and apply it to the mortgage principal balance in addition to making your normal mortgage payment.
3. If you have $3,000 in cash flow a month, pay $3,000 each month to pay down the HELOC.
4. In three months, the HELOC will be paid off. Do this process again until the property is paid off.
5. Then you will have increased cash flow and you can do this with an increased amount on another property.

Always be on the lookout for the right time to

1. refinance;
2. raise rents;
3. sell;
4. buy.

CHAPTER 6

INVESTMENT

Real estate is a great investment!

Remember what John Stuart Mill said: "Landlords grow rich in their sleep."

If you buy the property right (below market value), use the rent to pay off the property, maintain the property, and reap the cash flow (always make sure there is a positive cash flow), you will be on the beach or achieve your dream in no time.

Here are some tips for investing in real estate:

1. Do your homework. Know the area and the comps.
2. Buy the property right (below market value).
3. Buy in the right location (in a good school district, up-and-coming area, or desirable area).
4. Have an exit strategy. Know when and how you want to get rid of the property.
5. Consider the holding costs and cash flow.
6. Use the same products and contractors as much as you can.

Real estate investing can be done part-time or on the side while you work another job.

Here are some goals you may want to consider:

1. Buy properties close to where you live.
2. Buy properties in areas you know well.
3. Manage properties yourself to save money. Hire a management company if you do not want this responsibility.
4. Set up the correct corporation and protection for your situation.
5. Analyze the deal thoroughly.
6. Consider the market conditions.
7. Determine your financing plan.
8. Develop a record-keeping process to account for items such as expenses, income, payments, contractors, contracts, and so on.
9. Monitor your investment and act accordingly based on the numbers.

Enjoy the Good Life and the Freedom when you
have accomplished the Items in the Book!

CHAPTER 7

REAL ESTATE RECORDS

Make a folder for each property that includes, at a minimum, the following items:

1. List of expenses
2. List of income
3. List of payments
4. Insurance information
5. Deed information
6. Indentures, if applicable
7. Mortgage information and statements
8. Correspondence
9. Receipts

Keep a real estate portfolio that includes the following items, at a minimum, for each of your properties:

1. Property address
2. Mortgage amount and closing date
3. Interest rate, mortgage term, refinance date, if applicable
4. Property fees, if applicable

5. Income
6. Cash flow (income and payment)
7. Value of the property
8. Lender loan number
9. Annual tax amount
10. Annual insurance amount

Keep a tenant list that includes, at a minimum, the following information for each tenant:

1. Property address
2. Tenant name(s)
3. Tenant(s) work and cell number(s)
4. Tenant(s) email address(es)
5. Lease start date
6. Lease end date
7. Date tenant has until to give notice of renewal or move

Keep a tax form for each property each year that tracks the following:

1. Income
2. Loan payment total
3. Interest paid
4. Insurance paid
5. Commissions paid
6. Cleaning and maintenance fees
7. Repair fees
8. Supply fees
9. Taxes paid
10. Utilities paid
11. Property or condo fees paid

You can then turn this tax form over to your accountant each year for each property, and all totals will be figured and ready to populate the federal and state tax forms.

CHAPTER 8

VALUE

Most properties increase in value over time. If this is the case, you may be able to refinance for a better rate or terms or take a HELOC or loan against the property. You can use the additional money as a down payment on another property.

This allows you to use tax-free money, earn interest on the extra money, as well as depreciate the asset for tax savings.

There are several improvements you can use to increase the value of a property:

1. Paint the inside.
2. Paint the outside.
3. Replace the flooring.
4. Add a carport.
5. Convert a carport to a garage.
6. Change hardware.
7. Replace curtains or blinds.
8. Install a garage door opener.
9. Add an alarm or security system.
10. Add a fence.

11. Replace the appliances.
12. Replace the roof.
13. Refresh or add landscaping.
14. Install or change light fixtures and fans.
15. Add a shed.
16. Add storage.
17. Add an irrigation system.
18. Add stone or brick on the property.
19. Add or update a deck or patio.
20. Add built-in bookshelves.
21. Add a window seat.
22. Add or update windows.
23. Add storage or built-ins to closets.
24. Install a skylight or sun tunnel.
25. Update bathroom(s).
26. Update the kitchen.

CHAPTER 9

SUCCESS

Strategies for Success

1. Be patient.
2. Keep personal and business accounts separate.
3. Buy medium or modestly priced properties.
4. Buy properties in great neighborhoods.
5. Assess value through the income stream that is generated.
6. Let others help.
7. Learn from your good and bad experiences.
8. Buy in areas you know well.
9. Buy below market value.
10. Do not overimprove for the house or market.
11. Factor in home owner association (HOA) fees.
12. Be proactive.
13. Take action.

Real Estate Success Attributes

1. Awareness
2. Patience
3. Firmness but kindness
4. Flexibility
5. Ability to make a decision
6. Toughness
7. Time management
8. Goal identification
9. Ability to take action

SECTION 2

REAL ESTATE GUIDE

CHAPTER 10

BENEFITS OF BEING A LANDLORD

Being a landlord can have many benefits:

1. Property paid for by tenants
2. Tax incentives and deductions
3. Cash flow
4. Appreciation
5. Replicable process with multiple properties
6. Continual passive income
7. Ability to use other people's money
8. Opportunity to live in the property or pass it on to your heirs
9. Ability for heirs to get the property at the stepped-up basis (current value at the time of possession)
10. Retirement funding

Remember people always need a place to live so landlords are always needed.

Design Your Dream Home and Your Dream Life!

RUNNING THE BUSINESS

Real estate can be a great investment, and you can borrow money to acquire it.

As part of your business, establish the following items and relationships:

1. Bank account for business
2. Post office box for correspondence and rent payments
3. Website, if applicable
4. Education to increase your knowledge
5. Accountant to handle taxes
6. Attorney to handle legal documents, evictions, and collections
7. Realtor to search for properties
8. Insurance agent
9. Contractors

Set aside money for unexpected costs, such as HVAC replacement or a leaky toilet. You will need reserves for maintenance, replacement, and emergencies.

Know the area you buy in. Consider a growing area and an area that is in demand.

Develop your goals for owning an investment property. Develop an exit strategy for your properties and your portfolio. Determine when to buy and sell, and what you want to leave to others.

Ensure contractors are insured and bonded. Buy at a discount and sell at retail. Make sure you protect your investments as well as your personal house, assets, and possessions.

CHAPTER 12

BUYING THE PROPERTY

Buy the property right!

I cannot emphasize this one enough. You have to follow the numbers and not overpay. Usually you would not pay more than 70–80 percent of retail value. Also ensure there is positive cash flow.

Buy the property in a great location that is close to where you live. Finance the property to get in and then pay it off as soon as you can by accelerating the payments.

FIXING UP THE PROPERTY

When using contractors, you want to build a relationship with them so they will respond when you need them. Treat them well and pay them promptly.

Improve the property for the type of house and the neighborhood. Do not overimprove.

SHOWING THE PROPERTY

Be careful when showing property, as you do not know the people coming and their motivations. If possible, have two people present for the showing. Keep your phone in your hand and have a trusted person on the phone just in case.

Give current tenants notice if you need to visit or show the unit. Usually twenty-four to forty-eight hours is sufficient; you can give even more notice if you can. Ask your tenant the best days and times to show the property and conform to this when possible. When showing up to your property, identify yourself with your name or by saying you are the property manager.

Before showing a property, take these steps:

1. Obtain the prospect's full name and phone number.
2. Look up the person on the internet or on a court website like Case-net in Missouri if your state has one.
3. Have your cell phone ready.
4. Have a friend in the vehicle, in the house, or on the phone.
5. Ask for photo identification.

Make sure you get city inspections, when required, when the property is vacant. Also apply for occupancy permits when required.

CHAPTER 15

FINDING TENANTS

Treat all prospects the same. Require interested parties to fill out and sign an application.

Take these steps to qualify tenants:

1. Check their credit report.
2. Do a background check.
3. Do a reference check.
4. Do an employment check.
5. Conduct a rental reference.

Have all prospects complete a tenant information sheet that may contain

1. property address;
2. name;
3. date;
4. phone;
5. email;
6. desired lease start date;
7. desired lease term;

8. reason for moving;
9. number of adults and children;
10. income (to judge if they meet your income requirement);
11. availability of security deposit and rent to move in;
12. smoking habits;
13. number and type of pets;
14. interest in lease-to-own option.

Ask all prospects the same questions. Having this form will help you remember them.

Do not take the property off the market until the lease is signed and the security deposit has been collected. You may want to require a cashier's check for the security deposit and required rent prior to move-in so you know you have the money.

Here is the process for finding a tenant and leasing the property:

1. Marketing
2. Prescreen
3. Showings
4. Application completion
5. Verification and approval
6. Offer
7. Completion of lease
8. Written expectations provided to tenant (these should also be in the lease)
9. Move-in walk through detailing the condition of each room, which the landlord and tenants should sign
10. Collection of remaining security deposit, pet deposit, or rent due prior to move in
11. Key exchange

Real Estate Investing Can Be Profitable!

CHAPTER 16

MANAGING TENANTS

Become familiar with your state's landlord and tenant laws. Depending on market conditions, you can raise rents over time.

Collect a fair security deposit and pet deposit. Always have a signed lease for your protection and the protection of your tenants. Copy checks when you receive them and record the rent that was paid and whether it was late or not. If the rent was late, record the date you received it, calculate the late fee, and notify the tenants.

Do not leave the maintenance of your property to your tenant under a normal lease. You may negotiate some maintenance items in a lease purchase, but you may want to check on items at least twice a year.

If the tenant does not pay at all or is behind, start the eviction process right away unless you have a payment plan worked out. However, once the tenant misses one of those payments, you probably need to start the eviction process. Usually when a tenant gets into trouble or falls behind, they cannot afford to live in your property. Waiting to file prolongs the inevitable, ultimately to the landlord's detriment in terms of loss of money and time. Send a late notice the day after the rent is due if you've not received it. Send a pay-or-quit notice a week after the rent is due if you've not received it. If you receive no response from the tenant, start the eviction process unless arrangements are agreed to in writing and followed.

When you turn over the property to a tenant, it should be clean and safe. Change locks and keys between tenants. Smart keys are great, as they enable the landlord to rekey without replacing the existing lock and do it in a matter of minutes. Tenants should carry renter's insurance, and this requirement should be in your lease. Ask for a copy of the declaration page from their renter's insurance documentation.

Respond to tenant issues or questions within twenty-four hours. This is being a responsive landlord and will generate goodwill between you both. Provide utility information to the tenant when you sign the lease so they can contact the providers to transfer the utilities into their name.

Require a written notice to vacate. When a tenant lets you know they are leaving at the end of the lease, determine the move-out walk through date and time and notify them about it in writing.

If your tenant leaves property behind, take an inventory and photos and contact them in writing to come get them. If they do not respond or want the items, you will have that in writing. Notify your attorney for further direction on whether you can get rid of the items or need to let a certain amount of time go by before getting rid of them.

Complete the move-out walk through, being sure to detail the condition of each room and any damages that occurred during tenancy. Complete and send a written security deposit refund letter within thirty days of the lease end or according to your state's requirements. This may include money refunded or no money if the tenant owes you money. Detail any money you withheld for what the tenant owes you and from their security or pet deposits.

You can manage your property and tenants or hire a management company to perform this function. If you hire a company, they should provide the following services:

1. Market the property.
2. Show the property.
3. Find and qualify tenants.
4. Negotiate the lease.
5. Collect rents.
6. Pay bills.
7. Keep records.
8. Send owner the stats of income and expenses and money owed.
9. Handle property maintenance.
10. Handle repairs.
11. Handle evictions.
12. Release the property when tenants move out.

Tenant pleasers include the following and should be used when applicable:

1. No rent increases
2. Modest rent increases
3. Responsiveness (usually within twenty-four hours)
4. Fixing issues promptly (usually within twenty-four to seventy-two hours)
5. Respect for tenant's privacy
6. Keeping the tenant informed
7. Friendliness
8. Appreciation
9. An annual walk through
10. Newsletter with offers, tips, and so on.
11. A welcome gift or note
12. Cards or gift cards (sent regularly)
13. Professionalism

Remember, tenant turnover can be expensive!
You want to retain good tenants!

NEGOTIATING THE LEASE

Make sure you always have all adult tenants sign a lease. You should also always collect a security and, if applicable, a pet deposit. A security deposit is normally one month of rent or more. The pet deposit should be tailored to replacement costs if damage occurs, as well as the number and types of pets.

I recommend including in the lease that it is the tenants' responsibility to get the carpets professionally cleaned, and requesting that they produce a receipt.

Research the market, and price the rental at market rate. Realize that vacancy is the enemy and you may want to consider offering a discount or reducing rent or the deposit to attract prospects if needed.

The following should be included in the lease:

1. Landlord and tenant names
2. Property address
3. Lease term and rent amount, including late fees and bounced check fees
4. Start and end dates

5. Where to send rent payments
6. Lead paint disclosure, if applicable
7. Renewal terms
8. Access, regular and emergency
9. Marketing rights
10. Security deposit amount and refund terms
11. Pet deposit amount and refund terms
12. Compliance with laws
13. Abandonment terms
14. Clause that lease is not assignable or cannot be sublet
15. Enjoyment terms
16. Surrender terms
17. Personal property terms
18. Maintenance terms
19. Tenant responsibilities, including smoke detectors, furnace filters, renter's insurance, utilities, exterior and interior care, locks, appliances, cleaning, and so on
20. Landlord responsibilities
21. How long a guest can stay
22. Time frame for giving written notice of vacating and fees associated if notice is not given on time (recommend thirty to sixty days' notice)
23. Holdover terms and fee
24. Eviction terms

All parties should initial each page of the lease and then sign and date at the bottom of the last page.

If the tenants are staying on after the lease's expiration, complete a lease extension and have all parties sign it.

If the tenants require any changes to the lease, complete an addendum to it and have all parties sign it.

Be sure to review replacement of batteries in smoke detectors and filters in furnaces with tenants and when this should be done.

Make sure the number and weight of pets meet local, state, and subdivision regulations.

LEASE AGREEMENT

_____, by and
_____ (Lessee).

This Lease Agreement ("Lease") is made as of the _____ day of _____
("Lessor") and
between _____

PREMISES. The Premises are known
occupied solely by the Lessee and t
purposes only, and not for purpose
possession of the Premises on thi

mises"). The Premises are to be used and
for single family residential
be li

LEASE TERM AND RENT:
and end on _____ without any
of $_____

Tenant Information Sheet

Property _____

Name _____

Date _____ Phone _____

Email _____

When are you able to start a lease? _____

How long of a lease? 1 Year   2 Years 3 or more Years

Why Moving? _____

How many people will reside in th

CHAPTER 18

MANAGING THE PROPERTY

There are two advantages of managing your own property:

1. There are no fees.
2. You make the decisions.

The downside to managing your own property is that you are on call 24-7 and you have to deal with emergencies and headaches.

On the other hand, there are three advantages of using a property management company:

1. The company fields calls.
2. The company handles the headaches.
3. The company handles emergencies.

The downside is the fees you pay to the management company.

Consider rental loss insurance in case of an accident, and umbrella insurance in case you are sued. Consider putting properties in an LLC for protection.

Maintain your property. Check on the property at least one to two times per year and handle anything that's not working. Improve the property as you can.

Never leave valuables in your rental property.

Consult a tax professional to help with depreciating properties and the best use for tax efficiency. As depreciation occurs, your cost basis decreases and this will need to be taken into account when and if you sell.

Record the move-in and move-out conditions of the property upon walk throughs, and have both the landlord and tenant sign this document. Keep track of mileage and other expenses for property-related activities, as these can be deducted on taxes. Take photos of any damage in your property and keep them on your computer or as hard copies.

CHAPTER 19

LANDLORD FINANCES

Record all general real estate–related expenses each year, total them, and give them to your accountant. Separate them by property.

If you have lived in a property two of the last five years, then you can sell the property within that time and avoid paying capital gains tax. If not, a 1031 exchange offers a tax-deferred benefit to get a similar or upgraded property. Refinance if it makes sense to lower your payment, get better terms, or get cash out to purchase or pay down another property.

Passive Income-Watch the Money Roll In!

CHAPTER 20

LANDLORD RECORDS

Meticulous records are a must! You need to record expenses and income.

Read and understand all documents you are considering signing.

Keep a folder on each property and a sheet or document for expenses, income, payments, and related papers such as mortgage statements, deeds, copies of rent checks, copies of checks written for maintenance or supplies, as well as all receipts for expenses or work done.

Keep a tenant list that includes the following information:

1. Date of original lease
2. Property address
3. Tenant name(s)
4. Tenant work and cell phone numbers
5. Tenant email address(es)
6. Lease expiration date
7. Date when tenant has to give notice of renewal or move out

Keep a real estate investment portfolio that includes a line for each property that details the following:

1. Property address
2. Mortgage amount
3. Owner
4. Property closing date
5. Insurance cost
6. Tax cost
7. Interest rate and terms
8. Payment amount, as well as HOA fee, if applicable
9. Income received
10. Cash flow
11. Value of the property
12. Lender name and number

Keep a tax form each year for each property that includes the following information:

1. Income
2. Loan payment total
3. Interest paid
4. Insurance paid
5. Commissions paid
6. Cleaning and maintenance fees
7. Repair fees
8. Supply fees
9. Taxes paid
10. Utilities paid
11. Property, HOA, or condo fees paid

Tax Form for Real Estate Properties

Property _____

Income	Loan Payments	Interest	Insurance	Commissions

Cleaning/ Maint	Repairs	Supplies	Taxes	Utilities	Condo Fees

46

APPENDIX A: GLOSSARY

adjustable-rate mortgage (ARM)—A loan in which the future interest rate may change.

after repair value (ARV)—The value of a property after work has been done.

amortization—The repayment terms of a loan, including the principal and interest.

appraisal—An estimation of a property's current market value.

appreciation—Increase in value.

capital gain—The taxable profit from the sale of an appreciated asset.

cash flow—Amount of money received from rental income minus the amount paid in a mortgage, purchases, and expenses.

cost basis—The value of the property equal to the original cost plus improvements and minus depreciation.

debt-to-income ratio—A ratio that determines whether your loan gets approved. (Your monthly credit report payments are divided by your monthly gross income to get a percentage. Normally you want 45 percent or less.)

deduction—An expense that can be written off against income for tax purposes.

depreciation—Loss of value; a deduction used to reduce the tax liability of the owner of a qualified property.

equity—The portion of real estate that is owned or paid off or down based on the market value of the property.

home equity line of credit (HELOC)—A loan secured against the equity in a property. (It is a second mortgage and must be paid back when the property is sold.)

investment—The outlay of money for income or profit.

landlord—The owner of real estate who rents property to others (a.k.a. lessor).

lease—An agreement between a landlord and tenant that details the terms of tenancy.

lease purchase—An agreed-upon price and terms to convey real estate between two parties. (Usually part of the rent is applied to the purchase and the owner sells to the second party the right to purchase the property at a future date.)

market value—The most probable price a property should bring in an open market when selling.

mortgage—A financing obligation in which the borrower agrees to pledge property to secure the debt on a promissory note or bond.

rate—Interest charged by a lender for the use of their money over a specified period of time.

refinance—An extension or restructuring of existing financing.

rent—Money paid for occupancy of a property.

security deposit—Sum of money given to secure an obligation such as the leasing of a property.

tax-deferred exchange (1031)—Deferment of capital gains through an exchange of real property or other like-kind property.

tenant—A person who pays rent to occupy real estate (a.k.a. lessee).

term—Period of time for repayment of a loan.

underwriting—The process to assess the eligibility of a customer to receive a product (e.g., capital, mortgage, credit, etc.).

If you are interested in working with a mentor, contact Linda Pretre at realestatementor20@gmail.com.